WHAT PEOPLE ARE SAYING ABOUT *LIFE AFTER PORN*

The pressure of ministry is real and if unattended can create extreme difficulty in the life and ministry of a leader. David Espinoza addresses this topic head on in this powerful and practical workbook. He creates a pathway for leaders to find freedom and to develop a healthy strategy to protect against the attacks that every person faces. I highly recommend you read this life changing workbook and apply what it says. It will lift you up and in some cases save you from unnecessary tragedy.

—Chris Sonsken, Avail author, founder of South Hills Churches, and Church Boom Network

I have known David Espinoza for all of his life; he is a gifted pastor and a wonderful leader. Like so many who have found themselves bound to the grappling addiction of pornography, there was a season in which David found himself fighting this battle. But he was set free! Seeing David on the other side of victory, I am thrilled to say that I have witnessed, firsthand, the power of God's grace and restoration in David's ministry. Using his own life experiences of finding freedom, wisdom from his postgraduate studies, and biblical references, David has tailored a workbook for other ministers and spiritual leaders who like in his past, find themselves battling pornography addiction, as a guide to help them find healing. His insights will not only inspire, but also instruct readers on how to be set free and to stay free from the bondage of pornography. I recommend this book and believe that it will confront ministers with the truth that it is possible to be set free!

—Rich Guerra, SoCal Network Superintendent

This is an excellent "how to" workbook for those new to recovery or for those choosing to dive deeper into their recovery journey. Through a combination of the 12-Steps, Scripture, and vulnerable sharing, the book engages the reader and promotes healing through challenging and thought-provoking questions. Pastor David uses his heart of a shepherd and his experience as an overcomer to guide those who are struggling with addiction to not only talk the talk but walk the walk.

—Shannae Anderson, Ph.D.
Clinical Psychologist in the Recovery Field for over 35 years

LIFE AFTER PORN

Copyright © 2024 by David Espinoza

Published by Arrows & Stones

All rights reserved. No portion of this book may be reproduced, stored in a retrieval system, or transmitted in any form or by any means—electronic, mechanical, photocopy, recording, scanning, or other—except for brief quotations in critical reviews or articles, without prior written permission of the author.

Scripture quotations marked KJV are taken from the King James Version of the Bible. Public domain. Scripture quotations marked NIV are taken from the Holy Bible, New International Version®, NIV®. Copyright © 1973, 1978, 1984, 2011 by Biblica, Inc.™ Used by permission of Zondervan. All rights reserved worldwide. www.zondervan.com. The "NIV" and "New International Version" are trademarks registered in the United States Patent and Trademark Office by Biblica, Inc.™ | Scripture quotations marked NKJV are taken from the New King James Version®. Copyright © 1982 by Thomas Nelson. Used by permission. All rights reserved. | Scripture quotations marked TLB are taken from The Living Bible copy- right © 1971 by Tyndale House Foundation. Used by permission of Tyndale House Publishers Inc., Carol Stream, Illinois 60188. All rights reserved. The Living Bible, TLB, and The Living Bible logo are registered trademarks of Tyndale House Publishers. | Scripture quotations marked NLT are taken from the Holy Bible, New Living Translation, copyright © 1996, 2004, 2015 by Tyndale House Foundation. Used by permission of Tyndale House Publishers, Inc., Carol Stream, Illinois 60188. All rights reserved. | Scripture quotations marked MSG are taken from THE MESSAGE, copyright © 1993, 1994, 1995, 1996, 2000, 2001, 2002 by Eugene H. Peterson. Used by permission of NavPress. All rights reserved. Represented by Tyndale House Publishers, Inc. | Scripture quotations marked GNT are from the Good News Translation in Today's English Version—Second Edition. Copyright © 1992 by American Bible Society. Used by Permission. Scripture quotations marked AMP taken from The Amplified Bible®, Copyright © 1960, 1962, 1963, 1968, 1971, 1972, 1973, 1975, 1977, 1995 by The Lockman Foundation. Used by permission. www.Lockman.org.

For foreign and subsidiary rights, contact the author.

Cover design by: Sara Young

Cover photo by: Nestor Escobar

ISBN: 978-1-964794-03-7   1 2 3 4 5 6 7 8 9 10

Printed in the United States of America

LIFE AFTER PORN

HEALING from

pornography addiction

using biblical principles

and the 12 steps

DR. DAVID P. ESPINOZA JR.

ARROWS & STONES

CONTENTS

Introduction...9

STEP 1   CHAPTER 1. **I AM POWERLESS**..........................23
I admit that I am powerless over pornography and lust—that my life has become unmanageable.

STEP 2   CHAPTER 2. **I BELIEVE**................................26
I believe that a power greater than myself can restore me to sanity.

STEP 3   CHAPTER 3. **I SURRENDER**............................30
I am making a decision to turn my will and life over to the care of God as I understand Him.

STEP 4   CHAPTER 4. **I AM SEARCHING MYSELF**..............35
I am making a searching and fearless moral inventory of myself.

STEP 5   CHAPTER 5. **I ADMIT**..................................42
I am admitting to God, to myself, and to another human being the exact nature of my wrongs.

STEP 6   CHAPTER 6. **CHANGE ME**..............................45
I am entirely ready to have God remove all these defects of character.

STEP 7   CHAPTER 7. **HUMBLE ME**..............................49
I am humbly asking Him to remove my shortcomings.

CONTENTS

STEP 8 — CHAPTER 8. **I AM WILLING TO RECTIFY** 54
I am making a list of all persons I have harmed, and I am willing to make amends to them all.

STEP 9 — CHAPTER 9. **I WILL RECTIFY** 58
I am making direct amends to such people wherever possible, except when to do so would injure them or others.

STEP 10 — CHAPTER 10. **I APOLOGIZE** 62
I will continue to take personal inventory and when I am wrong, I will promptly admit it.

STEP 11 — CHAPTER 11. **I PRAY** 65
I am seeking through prayer and meditation to improve my conscious contact with God as I understand Him, praying only for knowledge of His will for me and the power to carry it out.

STEP 12 — CHAPTER 12. **PAY IT FORWARD** 68
Having had a spiritual awakening as the result of these Steps, I will carry this message to others battling pornography and lust, and practice these principles in all my endeavors.

Conclusion 71

Congratulations on beginning your journey of recovery.

INTRODUCTION

A PERSONAL TESTIMONY

YOU HAVE PROBABLY TRIED TO stop using pornography before. Why will this time be different? It will be different because:

1. You will get to the root of the issues that drove you to pornography and lust in the first place.

2. You will involve others.

3. Sobriety and Recovery will become a new way of life for you, not an achievement or graduation.

Let me tell you a little bit about me. I first saw a pornographic magazine when I was 7 years young in 1974. My life would never be the same. At 18, I began a 12 Steps program called Sexaholics Anonymous. I was in it for 6 months. I wish I would have stayed with it, but I didn't. I will regret not using the tools I was given at the time for the rest of my life. I continued to struggle with pornography until the age of 31. In the meantime I had graduated from Bible college, married my wife, had 2 daughters, and became a minister.

However, due to my addiction and sexual sin, I was placed on a disciplinary status for 2 years. In these 2 years, aside from marital and personal counseling, I returned to the 12 Steps program SA (Sexaholics Anonymous). I began to do everything I should have done when I was 18. I wasted 13 years and damaged many relationships. Since then, I have been on a journey being sober, living in recovery, and making amends to people I have harmed. I pray that you will not waste any more time but that you will begin this journey too. God has great things in store for you.

I experienced certain challenges due to my life experience. I am a Latino Pentecostal minister. The Latino culture like any other culture has its strengths and weaknesses, however,

INTRODUCTION

machismo, lack of confrontation, not only plague the Hispanic culture; they also empower the spirit of pornography.

I am also a Pentecostal Jesus follower. This means that I believe in the outward manifestation of the Holy Spirit. Casting out demons, longer worship services, sermons and altar calls have been common in our tradition. Overnight miracles at the altar are sometimes an expectation versus a journey and process in recovery. I went to the altar many times looking for a miracle. My miracle came in the form of 12 Steps meetings, fellowship, and recovery tools. I met a God of grace in SA that I never met in my boyhood church.

I am also a minister. We as ministers, sometimes especially as Latino ministers want to be a lone ranger. This doesn't work in ministry and it doesn't work in recovery. If Jesus needed help carrying His cross, so do you and I. While this book is being written by a Mexican American for Latino ministers, this workbook can help anyone who wants to be set free from lust, pornography and sexual sin. This book can help because it will help you get to the root of your issues rather than continue to just deal with the fruit that keeps growing back regardless of how many times you cut it off. It will also help because you will be forced to involve other safe people in your recovery. It will work because you will partner with others for the rest of your life to stay sober as you help newcomers in their journey. There is freedom and healing for you in Jesus' Name!

KEY TERMS

THERE ARE A FEW THINGS that are important for you to understand in recovery. Here is a list of some key terms. They will help you traverse this new road. Please read them and pray before you begin the step work. I pray God's wisdom, discernment and illumination upon you.

12 STEPS
Based on Alcoholics Anonymous, 12 statements and 12 groups of questions, personal inventories, and practices that help the addict recover from addiction and stay sober.

ABUSE
This is the second step in the addiction cycle. Here a person has crossed from use and the pornography practice becomes more obsessive, the material and subject matter becomes darker, and the person begins to struggle at any attempts to stop. The person is now abusing the use of pornography.

ACT OUT
Every addiction has a climax. For the gambler it is to gamble, for the alcoholic it is to drink alcohol. For the pornography addict it is to see pornography and masturbate.

ADDICT
A person who has succumbed to the addiction cycle and is now obsessively and compulsively trapped.

ADDICTION
Addiction is the final stage of use and abuse. It is the fact or condition of being obsessed with a particular substance or process. It is a compulsive need to consume or practice something harmful. A person will experience detrimental withdrawal symptoms upon attempting abstinence.

CYCLE
Every addict has a ritual or a cycle that they follow when beginning a process that will lead them to act out. When first triggered, the addict begins this ritual and continues until the process is consummated.

DRY DRUNK
A dry drunk is a person that no longer acts out in their addiction (alcohol, drugs, gambling, pornography, etc.), however, they do not get to the root issues that drive them to addiction. They continue to have the same characteristics, responses and attitudes of a drunk.

LUST
An attitude demanding that a natural instinct serve unnatural desires.[1] More than sexual, it is spiritual. Enough is never enough.

---
[1] Sexaholics Anonymous, (SA Literature, 1989), 40.

KEY TERMS

PORNOGRAPHY
Printed, audio, visual or virtual material containing the explicit description or display of sexual organs or activity, intended to stimulate erotic rather than aesthetic or emotional feelings.[2]

RECOVERY
The state of the addict in the process of obtaining sobriety and inner healing.

RECOVERY MEETINGS
A safe place where people meet to work the 12 Steps, bring to light current experiences, keep each other accountable and support each other.

RECOVERY MINISTRY
A ministry that focuses on helping free and heal the addict both from the compulsive behavior patterns and the maladaptive thinking that led the person to addiction.

SA
This abbreviation for Sexaholics Anonymous will refer to the 12 Steps program, not the book *Sexaholics Anonymous.*

SOBRIETY
The state of being sober, not affected by lust, not drunk.

TRIGGERS
Triggers are the emotional, mental, physical, sexual, social, spiritual and visual experiences that the addict has that can detonate and begin the addiction cycle. These could be everything from a sexual commercial on television to a resentment that is conjured up.

USE
The recreational practice of pornography that has not entered the areas of abuse or addiction. Here a person can stop using pornography without a struggle. This is usually the first step.

---

[2] Castro R, Fernando, "Remarks on an Unlikely Angelology," Literal Magazine, April 1, 2015, https://literalmagazine.com/remarks-on-an-unlikely-angelology/.

A LINEAR PROCESS OF ADDICTION

WE ALL HAVE CORE MATTERS and or unresolved issues that we are either ignoring, trying to work out, or suffering. These are the ROOT CAUSES of our addictions. These root issues can be resentment, trauma, and someone we do not forgive. When these root causes are not dealt with, many of us turn to different things and people to numb the pain. Some people turn to LUST for temporary relief. They will USE pornography to diminish bad memories and resentment. After a while this use turns into ABUSE. The abuse then turns into ADDICTION. Life begins to come apart. Some people become alarmed and either on their own or by the prodding from others, they seek help. Some just try and stop on their own. They experience at least temporarily some SOBRIETY. However, even if they can stop, if they do not seek recovery, they become a DRY DRUNK. They are the same person minus their drug of choice. Hopefully this person can see that they not only need to be sober but also be in RECOVERY and work on the root issues that took them to addiction in the first place. This recovery can take place through this workbook, recovery meetings and with the help of people in recovery.

QUIZ: IDENTIFYING IF THE PERSON

PLEASE TAKE THIS QUIZ. If you score 4 or more, you are probably an addict.

20 SEXAHOLICS ANONYMOUS QUESTIONS TO DETERMINE IF THE PERSON IS A SEX ADDICT.

1. Have you ever thought you needed help for your sexual thinking or behavior?
   YES / NO

2. That you'd be better off if you didn't keep "giving in"?
   YES / NO

3. That pornography and or masturbation are controlling you?
   YES / NO

4. Have you ever tried to stop or limit doing what you felt was wrong in your sexual behavior?
   YES / NO

5. Do you resort to pornography to escape, relieve anxiety, or because you can't cope?
   YES / NO

6. Do you feel guilt, remorse or depression afterward?
   YES / NO

7. Has your pursuit of pornography become more compulsive?
   YES / NO

8. Does it interfere with relations with your spouse?
   YES / NO

9. Do you have to resort to images or memories during sex?
   YES / NO

10. Does an irresistible impulse arise when you have an opportunity to see pornography
    YES / NO

IS A PORNOGRAPHY ADDICT

11   Do you keep going from one "relationship" or lover to another?

YES / NO

12   Do you feel the "right relationship" would help you stop lusting, masturbating, or being so promiscuous?

YES / NO

13   Do you have a destructive need – a desperate sexual or emotional need for someone, for sex, or for pornography?

YES / NO

14   Does pursuit of sex or pornography make you careless for yourself or the welfare of your family or others?

YES / NO

15   Has your effectiveness or concentration decreased as pornography and masturbation have become more compulsive?

YES / NO

16   Do you lose time from work for it?

YES / NO

17   Do you turn to a lower environment when pursuing sex or pornography?

YES / NO

18   Do you want to get away from pornography as soon as possible when the act is over?

YES / NO

19   Although your spouse is sexually compatible, do you still masturbate or have sex with others?

YES / NO

20   Have you ever been arrested for a sex-related offense?[3]

YES / NO

---

[3] *Sexaholics Anonymous*, (SA Literature, 1989), 8.

THE SPONSOR

THE SPONSOR IS KEY TO a person's recovery. The sponsor is a safe person with whom the addict can confide and seek advice. The sponsor is available for the workbook participant to contact when he or she is struggling to act out or is being triggered. The sponsor also helps walk the addict in recovery through the 12 Steps. The sponsor is familiar with addiction, sobriety, and recovery because the sponsor is still on his or her own journey of recovery. You will need a sponsor to complete this workbook. In the meantime you can ask a ministry peer or a spiritual authority in whom you can confide.

You are encouraged to find a sponsor with more time of sobriety than your own. Also, you are encouraged to obtain a sponsor of the same gender as your own, unless a same sex sponsor would be a trigger or temptation for you. Personal issues and details of a sexual nature are discussed with your sponsor. It is important to maintain healthy boundaries between the sponsor and the person being sponsored from the start.

When you believe that you are ready to sponsor someone, discuss it with your sponsor. They will be honest with you and give you advice on areas that you can improve to be the best sponsor you can possibly be. You are highly encouraged to plan on sponsoring someone for the rest of your life. This will keep you sensitive, aware and vigilant to addiction, sobriety and recovery in your own personal life. As Dr. Jesse Miranda said, "We all work best under a Paul, making ourselves accountable to a peer Barnabas, and mentoring a Timothy".

Qualities to look for in a sponsor and qualities to possess as a sponsor are first

1) COMPASSION. It is important to feel empathy with those that you will lead and help.

2) DISCRETION. You know that this person can keep a secret and will keep all you share with them confidential. They are your confidante.

3) NON-JUDGMENTAL. One of the reasons we never opened up to others about our struggle with pornography was for fear of being judged. While this person will not condone what you do, they will accept you, love you, and not judge you.

4) SPIRITUAL. This person is a person of prayer and God's Word, in knowledge and practice. This person will give you sound godly advice.

Sound advice avails us nothing unless we heed the advice. Listen to your sponsor. By asking for their help and advice, our ego begins to become deflated. This is a great step in recovery. We realize that we do not know everything about everything; that there are wiser people out there and they can help us. They help us when we reach out to them. It is not their responsibility to reach out to us. I am the one that needs help with my recovery and character. The mature sponsor knows that the recovering addict will need other people involved as well and encourages the participant to go to meetings and establish relationships with other recovery people.

Addicts can also be codependents. Pornography ruins relationships by promoting isolation, while at the same time forming sick dependency relationships with unhealthy people. The sponsor does not want to become a god for the one being sponsored. The addict must take ownership of their recovery. Rather than always giving the newcomer advice, a more prudent and effective method to mentor the recovering addict would be to involve coaching questions. As the addict seeks advice, respond with questions such as: Looking back, how would you handle things differently? What did you learn from this? What do you need to do to finish your next step? When will you do this? Who can help you through this? Etc.

You can find a sponsor. Ask God to lead you to the right person. See if you know of another minister with 12 Steps experience. You can humble yourself and ask a person in your congregation; possibly one of your leaders who has been in Alcoholics Anonymous or Celebrate Recovery. You can also look into local chapters of Sexaholics Anonymous. It is imperative for you to have a sponsor. Your first season without your drug of choice can leave you empty, cranky, vulnerable, and confused. You need help from someone who has been there. Get a sponsor!

Who will you ask to be your sponsor? When will you ask them?

HOW TO USE THE WORKBOOK

INDIVIDUALLY: It is important for you to find a sponsor. You need a sponsor to effectively complete the workbook. You will need to go over the recovery questions with your sponsor. So, read the introduction. Then start with Chapter 1 which is Step 1. In each chapter, read the Step and memorize it. Read the Scriptures and Thoughts. Then read the portion: *Going Deeper.* Think about these parts of the chapter, then start responding to the Recovery Questions. Take your time, but set a timeline for completing each chapter; one day, one week, 2 weeks, etc. At the end of each chapter go over your answers with your sponsor. Even though you might complete the workbook individually, you are highly encouraged and admonished to join a recovery group.

IN A GROUP: There are different options for completing the workbook as a group. It can be done by meeting weekly and filling it out privately yet together. A group can also fill it out during the week and then come back and discreetly share some of their findings and experiences. Answering the questions can be a very draining and scary experience. It is best to complete the workbook with a fellowship and network of peer support. The workbook can also be done during a weekend away at a retreat.

MEETING PROCEDURE AND ETIQUETTE

SHOULD YOU DECIDE TO BEGIN a recovery ministry or get together as a group and go through the workbook, here are some guidelines to help you have effective healthy meetings.

MEETING FORMAT

Anyone with over 30 days of sobriety can volunteer to facilitate the meeting. This person will call on raised hands as people wait their turn to speak. The goal is a 1 hour meeting. A typical meeting might follow this order ...

Opening Prayer, this could be a Step Prayer taken from AA (Alcoholics Anonymous), or The Serenity Prayer, The Lord's Prayer, or a prayer from the heart of one of the participants.   (3 minutes)

Readings, Scripture, material from AA, SA and other 12 Steps and Christian recovery ministries such as Celebrate Recovery or Overcomers Outreach.   (5 minutes)

Business, the secretary can give any program related announcements such as a member who called and cannot make it, an announcement about a recovery seminar, gathering, convention, etc. Also if a meeting will be canceled soon, this is the time to mention it. This is also the time to make financial donations. It is good for ministers to make financial donations. They do not always have the opportunity to give in worship services. Giving is the contrary action that needs to be implemented to counter the spirit of taking from others.   (5 minutes)

Chips, chips are given out and celebrated for various amounts of time of sobriety during the meeting. The facilitator asks if anyone is celebrating a certain amount of months or years.   (3 minutes)

Share Time, this is where everyone shares. Depending on the size of the group everyone should take 3-5 minutes to talk to ensure that everyone gets a chance to speak if they so desire. See Meeting Etiquette for what to share.   (40 minutes)

Closing Prayer, here everyone forms a circle, holds hands, and recites the same prayer together (Serenity Prayer, Lord's Prayer, Step Prayer), after this the group says together, "Keep coming back, it works if you work it and you're worth it".   (3 minutes)

AFTER THE MEETING, it is important that all ministers do these 2 things:

Stay and help clean up and put the chairs away. Ministers are used to being served. It is good for ministers to help serve.

It is important for ministers to stay and fellowship after the meeting. This will begin to break the power of isolation.

SERVICE POSITIONS

HERE ARE SOME OF THE ways that a person can sign up to serve and in doing so fortify their commitment to attend the meetings regularly.

- CHIPS, a person will keep a variety of sobriety chips to pass out at meetings. Some chips are the Newcomers Chips, 30 Days, 60 Days, 90 days, 6 months, 1 year, 18 months, 2 years, etc.

- COFFEE, someone can be in charge of having coffee ready before the meeting.

- SNACKS, someone can have snacks ready before the meeting.

- PHONE LIST, someone can be in charge of maintaining a group phone list.

- CHAIRS, someone can be in charge of setting up the chairs before the meeting begins.

- SECRETARY, someone can be in charge of keeping any kind of records and group information.

- TREASURE, someone can be in charge of keeping the group funds collected during meetings and possibly making a donation or pay rent to the host facility.

- LITERATURE, someone can be in charge of keeping a stock of workbooks and other recovery literature and books such as the *White Book* from SA.

MEETING ETIQUETTE

PERSONAL INTRODUCTION. WHEN IT IS your turn to share, introduce yourself by your first name and the initial of your last name. Then state that you are a recovering addict and share the amount of sobriety you have. For instance: *Hello everyone, David E here. I am a grateful recovering addict. I've been sober for 15 years.* This consistent confession will keep you humble and on point.

What do we share? Share time is a time for you to speak to the group concerning where you are in your recovery, how you feel, victories and defeats since the last time you met, and any lessons you have learned. Please, no graphic details and don't use other people's names.

We can only speak for ourselves. Speak in the *I*. Don't offer anyone advice unless they ask you for it.

No cross talk. Cross talk refers to engaging in a conversation with someone during a meeting. Raised hands are the best policy.

Anonymity is foundational to recovery ministry and recovery meetings. Do not give anyone's phone number out to anyone. The list is strictly for those that participate in the recovery ministry.

It is encouraged to address each other by first name only. This maintains anonymity. It also keeps everyone on the same playing field even. No pastor, doctor, or any other titled professional is higher than anyone else, especially at recovery meetings. The ground is level at the Cross of Christ.

Arrive on time, it is disrespectful to arrive late for a recovery meeting. Ministers can use their ministerial position to excuse tardiness. Others might assume that the good minister was off visiting someone at a hospital, praying, or studying. This is rarely the case when a minister is late for a meeting or an event. Tardiness is a bad habit. Arrive on time.

Give, it is important for the minister or spiritual leader to financially contribute at recovery meetings. He or she is sowing into their own recovery and the recovery of others. The addicted minister has been a taker and is now learning how to be a giver.

MEETING ETIQUETTE

Recovery Questions. The majority of the recovery step questions are taken from *Working the Steps with Carol R.*[4]

As you begin a new life of sobriety and recovery with a network of support and encouragement from others in recovery, consider St. John's words to us.

1 JOHN 1:6-9, *If we claim to have fellowship with him and yet walk in the darkness, we lie and do not live out the truth. But if we walk in the light, as he is in the light, we have fellowship with one another, and the blood of Jesus, his Son, purifies us from all sin. If we claim to be without sin, we deceive ourselves and the truth is not in us. If we confess our sins, he is faithful and just and will forgive us our sins and purify us from all unrighteousness.*

---

[4] Working the Steps with Carol R. https://sites.google.com/site/slysna/home

CHAPTER 1

STEP 1 *I admit that I am powerless over pornography and lust—that my life has become unmanageable.*

SCRIPTURES AND THOUGHTS

ROMANS 3:23, *For all have sinned and fall short of the glory of God.*

Everyone is a sinner. Because sin has deeply affected us, we are continually being restored from sin. The Psalmist says that our souls are being restored (Psalm 23:3). This applies to clergy as well. The minister in recovery is going through a good process (Philippians 1:6). However, no one is immune to sin. Everyone needs to be on the lookout for it. God told Cain in Genesis 4:9 that when we do not do what is right, it is because sin is crouching at our door. We must rule over it. Ministers are not impervious to sin.

ROMANS 6:23, *For the wages of sin is death, but the gift of God is eternal life in Jesus Christ, our Lord.*

The White Book of Sexaholics Anonymous says something similar. It states that the wages of lust is one's life.[5]

All our actions have consequences. Some are not as severe as others. Sin brings devastating consequences. It brings death, and death brings separation. Pornography separates and isolates its users from those around him or her. But there is healing, freedom, hope and recovery in fellowship with Christ and other Christ followers.

ROMANS 7:15, *I do not understand what I do. For what I want to do I do not do, but what I hate I do.*

None of us really get us. We truly are powerless. If Saint Paul struggled to understand himself and understand why he did what he didn't want to do, and not do what he wanted to do, so will we. However, the 12 Steps begin to shed light on what we do and why we do it.

MATTHEW 5:3, *Happy are those that know they are spiritually poor.*

Blessings and happiness come from admitting our shortcomings. It is only until we admit that we are powerless that we begin to search for a power greater than ourselves. We previously turned to lust and pornography to relieve our burdens. However, we found this false remedy to be even a more cruel slave master than the burdens themselves.

---
[5] Sexaholics Anonymous, (SA Literature, 1989) 19.

G O I N G

ADMITTING THAT WE ARE POWERLESS does not come easy for anyone. Denial does it's best through justifications and blaming others to deflect that we are really the problem. However, we are powerless over self and sin. Admitting this is a great starting point to recover from lust and pornography.

RECOVERY QUESTIONS

1. Have you seriously damaged your relationships with other people because of your addictive behaviors? If so, list the relationships and how you damaged them.

2. If other people have told you how you have hurt them, then write down what they said.

3. If your addictive behavior contributed to excessive spending, describe the situations and why you did it.

4. Describe times that you have withdrawn from social interaction and isolated yourself to an extreme degree, and why.

5. Describe incidents where you expressed inappropriate anger towards other people.

6. Describe embarrassing or humiliating incidents in your life. Were they related to your addictive behaviors? If so, how were they related?

DEEPER

7 Describe attempts that you have made in the past to control your addictive behaviors. How successful have they been? How do these attempts show the powerlessness that you have over your addictive behaviors?

8 Do you feel any remorse from the ways that you have acted in your life? If so, explain that in detail.

9 Describe any irrational or crazy thinking or events that have happened since you began your addictive behavior. Did you rationalize this thinking or behavior? If so, in what way?

10 Can you pinpoint one time period in your life when your life began to become extremely unmanageable? If so, describe that period of time and what was happening.

11 How would you summarize the powerlessness and unmanageability of your life in the face of your addiction?

12 Now go over your answers with your sponsor or the person that is helping you.

CHAPTER 2 — I BELIEVE

STEP 2 *I believe that a power greater than myself can restore me to sanity.*

SCRIPTURES AND THOUGHTS

JOHN 8:31-32, *To the Jews who had believed him, Jesus said, "If you hold to my teaching, you are really my disciples. Then you will know the truth, and the truth will set you free."*

Believing is the first step to being set free. It is part of the process. As Jesus told His followers, they must:

1. Believe in Him
2. Hold to His teachings
3. Be involved in discipleship
4. Then they will know the truth
5. Then the truth will set them free

First, a person must believe that God can use these 12 Steps and a recovery ministry to be set free. Second, this person seeking sobriety and recovery must hold to and practice these principles in all their life situations. Third, this person must be involved in a fellowship of recovery and have a sponsor. Fourth, this person will begin to learn new truths. Last, this person will eventually see these new truths manifest themselves in a new lifestyle, new behavior, and new habits.

EPHESIANS 3:20, *Now to him who is able to do immeasurably more than all we ask or imagine, according to his power that is at work within us*

God is not limited by your imagination. Believe that He can do more than you can imagine or understand. We must be open to the thought that God has a better way of doing what we need Him to do.

HEBREWS 11:6, *And without faith it is impossible to please God, because anyone who comes to him must believe that he exists and that he rewards those who earnestly seek him.*

Taken from AA, that God could and would if He were sought.[6] It is crucial for a person to believe not only that God can help them, but also that He wants to help them.

---

[6] *Alcoholics Anonymous Big Book*, 4th ed. (New York, NY: Alcoholics Anonymous World Services, 2002), 184.

GOING

THE TERM POWER IS INTRODUCED in this step. The Latino minister that is battling lust and pornography is familiar with this term power. Sometimes, the Latino minister is empowered and idolized. This is very dangerous. It is not healthy and opens the door to not being accountable to anyone. However, that illusion of power leaves the minister empty. More false power is sought in lust and pornography. This false god disappoints even more. All this is crazy thinking, especially for a clergy member that knows the truth.

In this step, the addict allows God's power to restore him or her to sanity; to right biblical thinking. God's power sets us free from sin. God's peace sets us free from fear. God's forgiveness sets us free from shame. God's truth sets us free from pornography's cunningness, deceit and insanity and restores us to sanity. As Paul tells us in 1 Corinthians 2:16, *for we have the mind of Christ.* Put Christ's mind to good use.

RECOVERY QUESTIONS

1. What was the religion that your family of origin practiced or claimed to be a part of?

2. List the positive and negative aspects as you see it of your family's religion.

3. Have you made a break with your family's religion, or have you stayed with it? Explain why you have taken your particular course of action.

DEEPER

4 Describe events, situations or people who have helped you to understand what a "Higher Power" or God is all about.

5 Describe any dreams that you have had about a "Higher Power" or God, and what they mean to you.

6 What have been your previous experiences with religion? How do you think that this does or does not relate to your experience with God as you understand God?

7 What are some ways that your culture and ethnicity have affected how you see God?

8 Most ministers believe that they have a better understanding of God than other people. What are some new things that you have learned about God through recovery that you didn't know before?

9 What are some misconceptions you had of God or of "Church" or of "Ministry" that you have discovered now that you are in recovery?

Now go over these answers with your sponsor or the person that is helping you.

CHAPTER 3 — I SURRENDER

STEP 3 *I am making a decision to turn my will and life over to the care of God as I understand Him.*

SCRIPTURES AND THOUGHTS

REVELATION 3:20, *Here I am! I stand at the door and knock. If anyone hears my voice and opens the door, I will come in and eat with that person, and they with me.*

Christ will come in and do His work if we open the door of our heart and our will. This is a decision. It is thought out. It is proactive. The addict has been very reactive and does not think things out, not weighing out the consequences of his or her actions. But this is a sound decision. The consequences of this decision will produce some of the best results that the recovering addict has ever experienced.

PHILIPPIANS 2:12-13, *Therefore, my dear friends, as you have always obeyed—not only in my presence, but now much more in my absence—continue to work out your salvation with fear and trembling, for it is God who works in you to will and to act in order to fulfill his good purpose.*

God is willing to do His part. We must be willing to do our part. The White Book of Sexaholics Anonymous states, "Without God, I can't; without me, God won't."[7]

In this step, the person is turning their will over to God in exchange for His will. As Paul tells the Philippians, we must work out our salvation because God wants to fulfill His will and act in our lives to fulfill His good purposes in us and through us.

---

[7] *White Book of Sexaholics*, 96.

GOING

HERE THE MINISTER IS TURNING over his or her will and life to the care of God. 1 Peter 5:7 tells us to cast our cares on God because He cares for us. This is difficult to accept for the minister that battles pornography use for a few reasons. First, the minister feels guilty for using pornography and is not sure if God will care for him or her due to sin. Second, the minister has probably dealt with shame, insecurity and feelings of inadequacy their whole life. It is difficult to believe that God will take care of him or her with these thoughts and feelings of not being good enough. Third, some Hispanic congregations and ministers border on the legalistic side. It is an environment more of good works rather than grace. Where no grace has been given to others when they fall, no grace will be expected. Last, sometimes it is difficult for the minister to begin the process of repentance, confession and restoration because of fear that they will lose their job and so lose their financial income. If the addicted clergy would just realize that God cares for them, they will trust Him through the whole process.

God as we understand Him. 12 Steps is not always popular in Hispanic congregations, especially Pentecostal congregations. Many parishioners and ministers came to the Lord, experienced instant sobriety, but never sought recovery; freedom and healing from the characteristics of an addict. Therefore, they don't see the need for any help outside the church or the Bible such as the 12 Steps or a recovery ministry. For some Pentecostals, the mentality is that a good altar call will fix everything. Everyone however understands God or their higher power differently. Working the 12 Steps will help the recovering minister understand God Jehovah in new ways. Working the 12 Steps will help the recovering minister understand the grace of God in new ways.

D E E P E R

RECOVERY QUESTIONS

1. What are your greatest fears about giving up control over your life to God as you understand God?

2. What things, people or circumstances have you tried to control in the past, and how has that turned out? Do you think that God will be able to handle your life better than you have?

3. How do you feel in general about turning your life over to God?

4. In what ways will you keep up the process of turning your life over to God? Possibilities include going to counseling, 12 Step meetings, meeting with others in recovery, writing a journal, service to others, meditation, reading, physical exercise, and staying in contact with your sponsor.

5. How would you answer the question "Who am I"?

6. How would you answer the question "Who is God"? In other words, describe God as you understand God.

7. Describe who or what you trust and to what degree.

8. How do you think that you should live your life after giving your life over to the care of God as you understand God? What changes do you expect to make, and how will this look in specific detail?

I SURRENDER

GOING DEEPER

9 How do you plan to celebrate or honor this step of turning your life over to the care of God?

10 Describe any celebration or honoring activity that you have actually made in turning your life over to the care of God.

11 Now go over these answers with your sponsor or the person who is helping you.

CHAPTER 4

STEP 4 *I am making a searching and fearless moral inventory of myself.*

SCRIPTURES AND THOUGHTS

MATTHEW 7:3-5, *Why do you look at the speck of sawdust in your brother's eye and pay no attention to the plank in your own eye? How can you say to your brother, 'Let me take the speck out of your eye,' when all the time there is a plank in your own eye? You hypocrite, first take the plank out of your own eye, and then you will see clearly to remove the speck from your brother's eye.*

We must take a look at ourselves before we look at others. Our view of others is distorted until we take a good look at ourselves. We must keep our side of the street clean before we try to clean someone else's side of the street.

EPHESIANS 4:25-32, *Therefore each of you must put off falsehood and speak truthfully to your neighbor, for we are all members of one body. "In your anger do not sin": Do not let the sun go down while you are still angry, and do not give the devil a foothold. Anyone who has been stealing must steal no longer, but must work, doing something useful with their own hands, that they may have something to share with those in need. Do not let any unwholesome talk come out of your mouths, but only what is helpful for building others up according to their needs, that it may benefit those who listen. And do not grieve the Holy Spirit of God, with whom you were sealed for the day of redemption. Get rid of all bitterness, rage and anger, brawling and slander, along with every form of malice. Be kind and compassionate to one another, forgiving each other, just as in Christ God forgave you.*

Scripture tells us what to do and what not to do; who and how to be and who and how not to be. This portion of the Bible speaks of a process of who we are becoming in Christ. It sets character and behavioral goals for us. It is easy for the busy minister to look at others yet not look at self. The Bible is a mirror. Let's take a good look. As we have worked on certain ministerial skills over the years, we must now learn how to work on our relational skills and character flaws.

GOING

ANY MINISTER IS USED TO helping others take a look at themselves. Occasionally the minister has to point out an area in the life of someone else that needs to be addressed. Taking a look at self is not common for anyone, let alone a minister, although it should be. For the minister that has a secret sin that they practice, it is common for them to keep their eyes fixed on other people so that they do not have to look at themselves.

As the addict begins to work on self, he or she will begin to experience healing and liberation from guilt and shame. Many times, guilt and shame are what the addict is attempting to medicate and numb in the first place. In *A Hunger for Healing,* J. Keith Miller points out that some of the traits that kept the addict alive and protected as a child are now killing the addict's relationships.[8] It is in a recovery ministry, 12 Steps programs and hopefully the local church that addicts in search of recovery can find safe and loving people to show them these blind spots.

In Ephesians 4:25-32, Paul mentions two key instructions for anyone battling pornography. First, Paul says in verse twenty-eight that the one who stole should steal no more. Pornography is self obsessive. A person that begins to habitually see pornography becomes preoccupied and consumed with self. SA says, "First addicts, then love cripples, we took from others to fill up what was lacking in ourselves."[9] Pornography teaches a person to become a taker. Through recovery, this same person that took from others learns how to give to others.

Second, Paul says in verse thirty-one that a person must rid themselves of all bitterness. He says in verse thirty-two that we are to forgive others the same way that Christ has forgiven us. Forgiveness is important because resentment is the fuel for the fire of addiction. As the addict begins to forgive others, the power of addiction dissipates.

---

[8] Miller, J. Keith, *A Hunger For Healing: The Twelve Steps as a Classic Model for Christian Spiritual Growth,* (Harper One, NY, 1991), 61.

[9] *Sexaholics Anonymous,* (SA Literature, 1989), 203.

D E E P E R

RECOVERY QUESTIONS

1. Have you had any broken relationships? If so, describe them and how they hurt others or yourself. Describe any grudges, anger or resentment that you have over these relationships.

2. Have you ever felt self-righteous? Explain when and the circumstances. Was this justified?

3. What events or triggers have caused you to begin your addictive behaviors in the past? Describe situations, feelings, events, food or people that you seem to be a part of your life just before or during your addictive behaviors.

4. Have you ever held a grudge? Did you try to get revenge? If so, explain the situation and how it played out, including whether or not someone else was hurt.

5. Describe times that you have been oversensitive. Did this ever damage your relationship with others, or were you just trying to keep your own boundaries?

6. Describe the faults that you most detest in others. Do you have any of these traits yourself?

GOING DEEPER

PUT A CHECKMARK BESIDE ANY of the following traits that you despise in others. Also check whether you see these traits in yourself.

TRAITS THAT I DESPISE IN OTHERS

TRAIT	IN OTHERS	IN MYSELF	TRAIT	IN OTHERS	IN MYSELF
Selfishness			Greedy		
Cowardice			Snobbish		
Dishonesty			Sarcastic		
Fearfulness			Hypercritical		
Controlling			Gossip		
Manipulative			Tightwad		
Intimidating			Harsh		
Power-hungry			Unforgiving		
Possessive			Verbally abusive		
Prejudiced			Physically abusive		
Overly dependent			Sexually abusive		
Procrastinating			Impatient		
Judgmental			Adulterous		
Preoccupied			Sneakiness		
Lying			Ungrateful		
Cheating			Cynical		
Intolerant			Bitter		
Self-Pitying			Full of Rage		
Jealous			Envious		
Insecure			Irresponsible		

GOING DEEPER

7 Have you failed to do things that you KNOW that you should have done? If so, then explain in detail.

8 Describe your relationship with your friends, co-workers or neighbors. Is there something that you wish that you could do over again? If so, explain in detail.

9 Describe your relationships with your family of origin. Do you have conflicts with any siblings or with your parents? Are you avoiding these matters in your family?

10 Describe the earliest memories of your life. Did you share a similar personality with those in your family, or were they very different from you? Do you think that these similarities or differences caused problems in your life? If so, explain.

11 If you were to describe your family's major themes, what would they be?

12 Describe your relationships with your nuclear family (spouse and children) if that is different now from your family of origin. Is there anything that you wish that you could erase from this part of your life?

13 Describe in detail any major experiences in your life that you believe changed your life forever afterwards (good or bad).

14 What decisions have you made in your life that made a significant impact on your life? How did you go about making those decisions?

GOING DEEPER

15 How much of your life have you used up already? If you drew a timeline of your life, where would you be now?

16 Put your major experiences and major decisions on a timeline. Is there a pattern of any kind?

17 What are you most ashamed of in your life?

18 Do you see any patterns in your addictive behaviors? If so, explain them in detail.

19 What have you done to cover and conceal your addictive behaviors? What other deceptions did this lead to?

20 What kind of personality do you exhibit at home? At school? At work? When no-one is around?

21 What is so shameful in your life that you would not want to tell anyone? Who would you hurt if you told this?

22 Write a summary of the highlights of your fourth step.

GOING DEEPER

23 How would you like to share your fourth step summary? What details would you like to make sure that are known? Write these details down in your summary and prepare the summary for presentation in your fifth step.

24 Describe any celebrations or honoring activities that you have done to honor the completion of your 4th step.

Now go over these answers with your sponsor or the person that is helping you.

CHAPTER 5 — I ADMIT

STEP 5 — *I am admitting to God, to myself, and to another human being the exact nature of my wrongs.*

SCRIPTURES AND THOUGHTS

JAMES 5:16, *Therefore confess your sins to each other and pray for each other so that you may be healed. The prayer of a righteous person is powerful and effective.*

Sometimes in the Latino culture, it is difficult and uncommon to open up to someone else. Direct access to and communication with God were sometimes overemphasized for those breaking away from the Roman Catholic Church. However, James tells us to confess our sins to each other, and we will experience healing. While we want to honor the Latino culture, we must embrace the culture of the Cross of Christ, obeying God's Word.

MATTHEW 7:15-20, *Watch out for false prophets. They come to you in sheep's clothing, but inwardly they are ferocious wolves. By their fruit you will recognize them. Do people pick grapes from thorn bushes, or figs from thistles? Likewise, every good tree bears good fruit, but a bad tree bears bad fruit. A good tree cannot bear bad fruit, and a bad tree cannot bear good fruit. Every tree that does not bear good fruit is cut down and thrown into the fire. Thus, by their fruit you will recognize them.*

Ministers who live double lives are wolves in sheep's clothing. In the Latino culture, much emphasis is placed on appearances and image. If the fruit looks good, such as being seen preaching, praying, visiting, etc. then the congregation assumes the root is good. Even the minister deceives him or herself that they are good, seeing self superficially in the sheep's clothing. Step 5 helps the addicted minister admit that they are a wolf at their core in need of help.

JEREMIAH 17:9-10, *The heart is deceitful above all things and beyond cure, Who can understand it? "I the Lord search the heart and examine the mind to reward each person according to their conduct, according to what their deeds deserve."*

In Step 5, the addict partners with God and another trusted person to take a look at him or herself. For years, the addict's heart has fooled themselves that everything is fine, or not that bad. This is an unhealthy and destructive attitude. While Step 4 deals with your actions, Step 5 deals with your attitudes.

GOING DEEPER

> ***THE EXACT NATURE OF OUR*** *wrongs.* An addict rarely takes responsibility for their harmful actions. But here the addict looks not only at what they do, but why they do it. The addict is selfish, immature, irresponsible, careless of others and self-centered. To admit this is a difficult thing to do. However, he or she has found a safe place in the workbook group and recovery ministry to confess their faults and find healing.
>
> The nature of wrongs is what is admitted and confessed to three persons: God, self, and another human being. They are specifically done in this order. It is only as life issues are addressed in this order that change can take place. A person must deal with God, then self, and then others. A person must receive God's love and forgiveness first, then love and forgive himself or herself, then he or she can truly love and forgive others. Not forgiving others is being ungrateful for our forgiveness. It is a character flaw. Other addicted ministers in a recovery ministry can be the safe other human beings with which to confess one's character flaws.

RECOVERY QUESTIONS

1. After working through the fourth step questions, what do you realize about your limitations and capabilities?

2. Describe any person who has helped you to see yourself more clearly and objectively in your process of recovery and of life.

3. What qualities would you like to have in a sponsor? How do the people in the list of possible sponsors measure up to these criteria?

4. Write down the names of the most trustworthy people that you know. Do you think that they would be willing or interested in being a sponsor for you?

I ADMIT

GOING DEEPER

5 Describe your feelings and expectations about sharing your fifth step with your sponsor.

6 List people that you can think of that you might share your story with. Write whether you think that they are a safe, risky or a bad choice to work your 5th step with.

7 Describe who you have chosen to be your sponsor and how they reacted when you approached them.

8 Describe what it was like in sharing the fifth step. How did you feel before, after and during the process? Are you glad that you have done this?

9 Describe any celebrations or activities that you have done in honor of completing the fifth step.

Now go over these answers with your sponsor or the person who is helping you.

STEP 6 *I am entirely ready to have God remove all these defects of character.*

SCRIPTURES AND THOUGHTS

ROMANS 12:1-2, *Therefore, I urge you, brothers and sisters, in view of God's mercy, to offer your bodies as a living sacrifice, holy and pleasing to God—this is your true and proper worship. Do not conform to the pattern of this world, but be transformed by the renewing of your mind. Then you will be able to test and approve what God's will is—his good, pleasing and perfect will.*

In these verses, we see God's desire to work in the whole person, both body and mind. The addict needs to let God do a holistic work in themselves. Mind and body; right-thinking will produce right living.

1 THESSALONIANS 5:23, *May God himself, the God of peace, sanctify you through and through. May your whole spirit, soul and body be kept blameless at the coming of our Lord Jesus Christ.*

The addict's spirit, soul and body have been damaged by lust, pornography and masturbation. Step 6 allows God to do a thorough restorative work in the workbook participant. The person is ready for God to remove all that He wants to remove.

GOING

THE MINISTER BATTLING PORNOGRAPHY must learn to be ready and present. As he or she is physically with others, the minister must discipline himself or herself to be emotionally, spiritually, and mentally present as well. Others notice that the minister is not fully present but might assume that their mind is occupied with other more important ministerial tasks or other congregants with more pressing issues. However, sometimes the minister is just thinking about their next high, a resentment, or how the person they are speaking with can serve a purpose in the minister's life. The minister in recovery will learn to be present in body, soul, and spirit.

The person is *entirely* ready for God to work. The addict goes through many "this is the last time." They do not always follow through on commitments to change or stop seeing pornography or masturbating. However, this time they are entirely ready because others are involved. They are now submitting themselves to a process, regardless of how painful that process will be.

RECOVERY QUESTIONS

1. Describe situations and events where you have been full of pride. What has this brought into your life that you like or enjoy? What problems has it caused you?

2. What are some healthy eating or exercise habits that you could start?

3. What are some unhealthy eating habits that you could give up?

D E E P E R

4 Describe some secret GOOD deeds that you have done or would like to do.

5 Describe situations and events where you have been greedy, overly needy or materialistic. What has this brought into your life that you like or enjoy? What problems has it caused you? Are you ready to give these attitudes over to the care of God?

6 Describe situations and events where you have given in to lust without regard for others or any morality. What has this brought into your life that you like or enjoy? What problems has it caused you? Are you ready to give these lustful feelings over to the power of God?

7 Describe situations and events where you have been dishonest. What has this brought into your life that you like or enjoy? What problems has it caused you? Are you ready to depend upon God to keep you from dishonesty?

8 Describe situations and events where you have given into excessive eating, drinking, shopping or covetousness. What has this brought into your life that you like or enjoy? What problems has it caused you? Are you ready to let God take control of these behaviors and attitudes?

9 Describe situations and events where you have been very envious or jealous of others. What has this brought into your life that you like or enjoy? What problems has it caused you? Are you ready to turn these situations over to God?

GOING DEEPER

10 Describe situations and events where you have avoided responsibility for your actions or lack of actions. What has this brought into your life that you like or enjoy? What problems has it caused you? Are you ready to allow God to help you take responsibility for your actions?

11 List your major defects of character.

12 What do you plan to do when these major defects of character begin to become evident? List each defect individually along with the proposed preventative behavior and how you will allow God to help you in your battle against these defects.

Now go over these answers with your sponsor or the person who is helping you.

CHAPTER 7

STEP 7 — *I am humbly asking Him to remove my shortcomings.*

SCRIPTURES AND THOUGHTS

PROVERBS 3:34, *He mocks proud mockers but shows favor to the humble and oppressed.*

Contrary to worldly advice that says that God helps those that help themselves; God helps the person that humbles themselves.

JAMES 4:6, *But he gives us more grace. That is why Scripture says: "God opposes the proud but shows favor to the humble."*

Recovery is first and foremost grace based. I met a God of grace in my 12 Steps program that I never met growing up in church.

1 PETER 5:5, *In the same way, you who are younger, submit yourselves to your elders. All of you, clothe yourselves with humility toward one another, because, "God opposes the proud but shows favor to the humble."*

We see 3 steps in Peter's words:

1. Submit yourself to someone more mature and with more experience (a sponsor).

2. Not only humble yourself before God; humble yourself also before those around you.

3. The result of these actions will open the door to God's favor upon you.

2 CORINTHIANS 12:8-10, *Three times I pleaded with the Lord to take it away from me. But he said to me, "My grace is sufficient for you, for my power is made perfect in weakness." Therefore, I will boast all the more gladly about my weaknesses, so that Christ's power may rest on me. hat is why, for Christ's sake, I delight in weaknesses, in insults, in hardships, in persecutions, in difficulties. For when I am weak, then I am strong.*

Certain privileges come from being a pastor. It is easy to become egocentric. Most addicts are takers and not givers. Step 7 states that we ask God to remove these shortcomings and character flaws because we have seen the damage they have caused in our lives and the lives around us.

True repentance is not promising God all that we will do. On the contrary, it is admitting what we are powerless to do. So, here, the addict asks God to do for them what they cannot do for themselves.

Paul pleaded with God three times to remove his thorn in the flesh. God told Paul that His grace was sufficient and that His power would be made perfect in Paul's weakness. One of the greatest lessons that the minister can learn: Victory comes through surrender.

SCRIPTURES AND THOUGHTS

The Latino minister wants to fight, battle, and wage war. We want victory now. However, victory over lust is progressive.

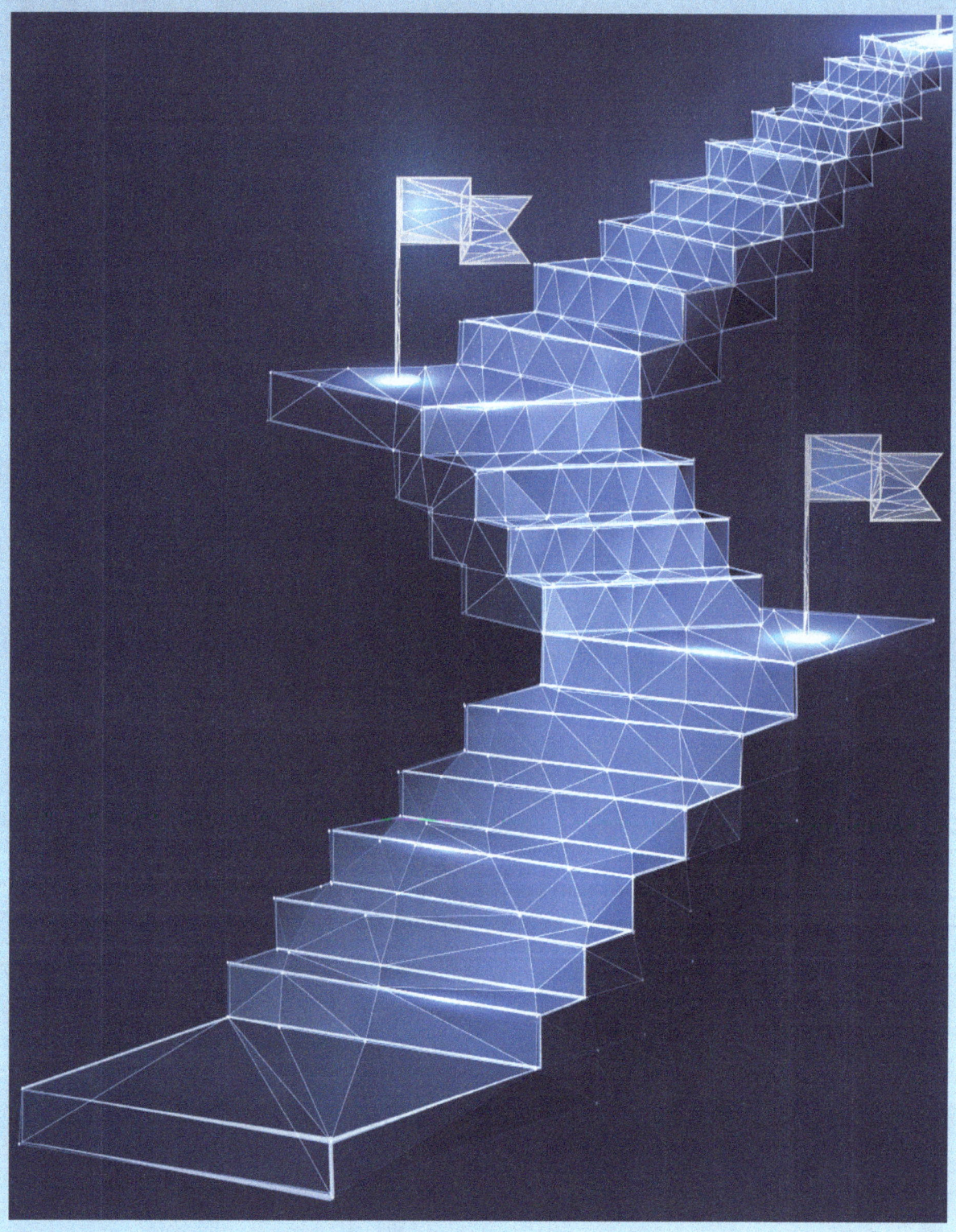

GOING DEEPER

SOMETIMES WHEN A PERSON EXPERIENCES an overnight miracle, they don't always appreciate it and or guard it. Nor can they explain what happened or how it happened with others in need of the same kind of miracle. Also, sometimes, people that stop drinking, using drugs or abusing pornography that experience an overnight miracle, don't always feel compassion for other people struggling with the same vice. They can be judgmental, thinking that if God did a miracle for them but not for the other person, the other person must not really want to be set free. Sometimes these people turn out to be "dry drunks". They are free from the addiction or sinful habit, but still have the characteristics of an addict.

However, when a person has been through a longer process like the 12 steps, they will appreciate the miracle. They will understand the steps and the hard work that had to be taken in order to experience sobriety as well as recovery. That person will be able to informatively share this process with others that are struggling. They will also feel compassion for other addicts, knowing what lies ahead of them. Typically, when a sober addict sees another addict and is triggered with shame or feels uncomfortable, they are still struggling themselves. But when a sober addict sees another addict struggling, and they feel compassion, it is because they are in recovery and God is working with them. God will get you there, too.

GOING DEEPER

RECOVERY QUESTIONS

1. What defects will be most difficult to give up? In what order do you plan to give them up?

2. What kind of situations, stressors or pressures cause you to regress back into your defects of character? What can you do to lessen the likelihood of that stress occurring?

3. Where do you feel most supported and helped in your striving for recovery?

4. What makes you lose hope? Can you avoid such situations? If so, then how?

5. What (person, situation, event, thought) restores your hope? Is there a way to maximize those influences? If so, then how?

6. What would you like to recapture in your life?

7. Describe in detail what you think that your life will be like with your defects of character removed from you.

8. What are you grateful for?

GOING DEEPER

9 When do you think that life has been especially good for you? When did you have the greatest joy?

10 Describe your typical day's activities in terms of how much time you spend on each type of activity.

11 Describe your typical day's activities if you knew that you had only one year to live.

12 Have you made the correct decisions about how to spend time with loved ones, in solitude and with your discretionary time? If not, how would you like to change it?

13 What would you do if you were granted three wishes?

14 What do you think that you can do to leave the world a better place and accomplish your mission in life?

Now go over these answers with your sponsor or the person who is helping you.

CHAPTER 8 — I AM WILLING TO RECTIFY

STEP 8 *I am making a list of all persons I have harmed, and I am willing to make amends to them all.*

SCRIPTURES AND THOUGHTS

PSALM 139:23-24, *Search me, God, and know my heart; test me and know my anxious thoughts.*

SEE IF THERE IS ANY OFFENSIVE WAY IN ME, *and lead me in the way everlasting.*

Here the psalmist opens himself up to the probing of God. This is what is done in Step 8. A search is made, not with the hope that nothing will be found, but that offensive ways can be pointed out so that the participant can come out a better person. The attitude is not "I hope they don't find anything." Rather, the addicted minister knows that character change is needed, so he or she is anticipating internal flaws to surface so that they can be addressed.

PSALM 51:3, *For I know my transgressions, and my sin is always before me.*

The key word here is "I." I am making a list. I have harmed people. I am willing to make amends. I know I have committed transgressions. I have sinned. This may seem scary and lonely. However, the person making the list does not have to do it alone. Step 7 mentions that God and other people in recovery will be involved to help the person through.

GOING DEEPER

THE FELLOWSHIP OF PEOPLE IN recovery is a safe place for the addicted minister to look back at all the people they have harmed. It is safe because others in the fellowship have gone down that road before. They understand the shame and regret of going through this process. They can be of great aid. However, they also offer another great benefit. They help the addict screen his or her apology, making sure it is sincere and focused on self, in no way blaming the other person.

The importance of this step is that the offender is taking ownership of their sin and selfishness. Repentance is required. However, if a person does not take ownership of the harm that they have caused, they will never repent. The apology is not "if I offended you in any way, I am sorry." The addict will apologize by stating what they did and saying that they are sorry for doing it.

GOING DEEPER

RECOVERY QUESTIONS

1. How have you hurt yourself by practicing your addiction?

2. What important relationships did you destroy or damage because of your addictive behaviors?

3. How much time and energy have you lost from your addictive behaviors? What do you think you would have done or become had it not been for your addictive behaviors?

4. Make a list of all those that you have possibly harmed by your addictive behaviors. List the effect on them as individuals and on your relationship.

5. Take the list of people that you have harmed and make a list of possible amends for each one of them.

6. From the list of possible amends, choose the ones that seem most appropriate, and mark them according to level of difficulty.

7. What consequences do you fear in making amends? What is the worst thing that can happen? What is the best thing that can happen? What is likely to happen?

8. Do you feel angry or resentful towards any people on your amends list? If so, write them a letter of anger, but don't send it to them. Describe here any other ways that you have used to get rid of the anger and resentment towards anyone on your list.

GOING DEEPER

9 Describe any dreams that relate to making amends to others.

10 Now go over these answers with your sponsor or the person who is helping you.

CHAPTER 9 — I WILL RECTIFY

STEP 9 *I am making direct amends to such people wherever possible, except when to do so would injure them or others.*

SCRIPTURES AND THOUGHTS

ROMANS 12:18, *If it is possible, as far as it depends on you, live at peace with everyone.*

With the same spirit of Step 9, a person ought to attempt to be at peace with everyone, especially with those that the addicted minister has harmed. This is not always possible. In some cases it is best to not offer amends because more damage and hurt could be done. Also, sometimes this person has died and there is no way to make direct amends now. However, all healthy attempts should be made to make amends and bring peace. Sponsors can offer suggestions of how alternative amends can be made.

MATTHEW 5:23-24, *Therefore, if you are offering your gift at the altar and there remember that your brother or sister has something against you, leave your gift there in front of the altar. First go and be reconciled to them; then come and offer your gift.*

Our worship is hindered when we have unresolved issues with other people. God wants us to make amends with those we have offended, and then come and worship Him.

1 PETER 3:7, *Husbands, in the same way be considerate as you live with your wives, and treat them with respect as the weaker partner and as heirs with you of the gracious gift of life, so that nothing will hinder your prayers.*

Our prayers are also hindered when we mistreat others. God wants us to treat others with respect. We are to treat other people, especially of the same faith and family, as co-heirs of God's grace. We are to grace others the same way God has graced us.

GOING DEEPER

THE ADDICT HAS TRIED TO control and manipulate others for years. That is the old way of life. As the addict makes amends with those they have harmed, they cannot control or manipulate the offended person's response. Here is where the recovering addict prays the Serenity Prayer:

God, grant me the serenity, to accept the things I cannot change; the courage to change the things I can; and the wisdom to know the difference. Apologize and leave it in God's hands.

As the participant begins to make amends with those they have harmed, a great load that they have carried for years begins to be lifted. The White Book of Sexaholics Anonymous says that when Step Nine is taken, there is a big burden released.[10] The addict begins to feel peace. They have peace with God, peace with self, and now peace with others. This is the order in which peace works. One must have peace with God, in order to have peace with self, and when one has peace with God and self, they can humbly make peace with others through amends.

---

10 *Sexaholics Anonymous*, (SA Literature 1989), 205.

GOING DEEPER

RECOVERY QUESTIONS

1. What amends do you think that you have already made? These can include apologies already made, helpful tasks for those that you have hurt, changed attitudes and so forth.

2. From your list of amends, if there are apologies that you need to make, write them down here first.

3. Read your apologies to a friend or a sponsor and ask them if it sounds sincere or if it sounds defensive or like an attack on the other person. Record here what response they have about them.

4. Role play with your sponsor or friends for anything that you are going to say when making amends. Record here how these practice sessions went and what you learned.

5. After you have had your first encounter with making amends, record what happened here. How did you feel about it? How did the other person respond? What have you learned from this? What would you do differently next time?

6. After you have done your first several encounters for making amends (for example, after 5 times of making amends), record your overall impressions here. Is there anything common? Has anything surprised you? Has anything disappointed you? How do you feel about the process and how has it affected you?

7. What amends do you have the most difficulty making? What do you need to do to be able to make these amends?

GOING DEEPER

8 How has making amends affected your relationship with others?

9 How are you dealing with the feedback from others after making amends? How are you feeling? How are you dealing with the desire to defend yourself?

10 Write down any other amends that you found that you needed to make after starting the process of making amends.

11 How can you celebrate or honor the completion of your making amends (step 9)

12 Have you had any dreams about making amends? If so, describe them in detail.

Now go over these answers with your sponsor or the person who is helping you.

CHAPTER 10 — I APOLOGIZE

STEP 10 *I will continue to take personal inventory and when I am wrong, I will promptly admit it.*

SCRIPTURES AND THOUGHTS

PSALM 23:4, *he restores my soul. He guides me along the right paths for his name's sake.*

The psalmist tells us that God is restoring our souls. Christian theology teaches us that the soul of a person is their thoughts, feelings and will. This is what God is restoring to sanity. That is God's part. The person in recovery's part is to admit when they are wrong; to admit when they are acting out and behaving in the old person's ways, habits, and behaviors. As God restores us, we begin to see more clearly when we are wrong and promptly confess and repent.

GALATIANS 5:16-21, *So I say, walk by the Spirit, and you will not gratify the desires of the flesh. For the flesh desires what is contrary to the Spirit, and the Spirit what is contrary to the flesh. They are in conflict with each other, so that you are not to do whatever you want. But if you are led by the Spirit, you are not under the law. The acts of the flesh are obvious: sexual immorality, impurity and debauchery; idolatry and witchcraft; hatred, discord, jealousy, fits of rage, selfish ambition, dissensions, factions and envy; drunkenness, orgies, and the like. I warn you, as I did before, that those who live like this will not inherit the kingdom of God.*

The person in recovery must live in the Spirit. One of the ways to do this is to practice the 12 Steps in every area of life. When the recovering addict practices these steps, they will not gratify the desires of the flesh. A daily inventory needs to be a lifelong practice for the workbook and recovery ministry participant. When the recovering addict sees that he or she is practicing anything even close to verse 19–21, it is time to confess and repent. It is time to call their sponsor or brother or sister in the program and admit that they are in the wrong.

EPHESIANS 4:22-24, *You were taught, with regard to your former way of life, to put off your old self, which is being corrupted by its deceitful desires; to be made new in the attitude of your minds; and to put on the new self, created to be like God in true righteousness and holiness.*

Paul lays out the process that the believer and the person in recovery are going through. The old person must be put off. The addict's old way of being must cease. New tools in recovery will bring new attitudes and new actions. The recovering addict is becoming like Christ.

GOING DEEPER

AS YOU PROGRESS IN RECOVERY, you realize that there is no graduation. You never fully reach becoming someone that has arrived or made it. Recovery is a lifelong process and a new way of being. The honeymoon with sobriety only is over and the marriage with recovery begins.

Step 10 is the pivotal link between sobriety and recovery. If a person does not make Step 10 a daily practice, then he or she will revert to the old person. Even if they never see pornography, get drunk, or gamble again, if they don't practice Step 10, they will plateau and remain a dry drunk.

Proverbs 3:7 teaches a person not to be wise in their own eyes. The recovering minister is now admitting when they are wrong. They are learning the art of learning from other's victories and defeats. As the recovering addict attends 12 Steps meetings and support groups, he or she gleans from other wiser people, promptly admitting when they are wrong. The recovering addict has found a safe place to confess one's faults and be healed.

GOING DEEPER

RECOVERY QUESTIONS

1 What is your plan to allow time for reflection each day?

2 What new behaviors would you like to practice in order to make your program more effective? How would you go about implementing these?

3 What kind of behaviors and attitudes do you need to be most vigilant against to keep from your addictive behaviors?

4 What are your triggers for addictive behavior? How can you guard against them or prepare for them?

5 What are some amends or remedies that you should make when you find out that you are wrong?

6 Who will you involve to keep you accountable? To whom will you promptly admit when you are wrong?

Now go over these answers with your sponsor or the person who is helping you.

CHAPTER 11

I PRAY

STEP 11 *I am seeking through prayer and meditation to improve my conscious contact with God as I understand Him, praying only for knowledge of His will for me and the power to carry it out.*

SCRIPTURES AND THOUGHTS

The Psalms are full of prayers and petitions to God seeking His help (Psalm 5:2), wisdom (Psalm 90:12), rescue (Psalm 17:13), and a plea for character change (Psalm 51:10). Jesus taught his disciples how to pray in Matthew 6:9-13. Paul prays over the Ephesians in chapter 3:14-21.

These examples pave the way for the recovering minister to pray without ceasing. Previously, the pornography addict was constantly thinking about lust and sexual images. Now, they make an effort to focus on prayer and God's Word day and night.

PSALM 1:2, *but whose delight is in the law of the Lord, and who meditates on his law day and night.*

The picture here is of a person meditating on God's Law. Previously, lust consumed the addict's mind. Now in recovery, that same mind is meditating upon Scripture and 12 Steps reading materials and principles. There was a mental lack of control with obsession, but now with meditation, there is a strategic mental focus.

PSALM 48:9, *Within your temple, O God, we meditate on your unfailing love.*

The picture here is of a group of people meditating on God's Law. This is symbolic of recovery meetings. Together, people in recovery are meditating upon God, biblical principles, 12 Steps literature, and a sober life.

GOING DEEPER

> **THE ADDICT HAS LIVED IN** his or her head for many years. They speak to themselves audibly and silently. In his book *The Gospel and the Twelve Steps*, Martin M. Davis encourages addicts in recovery, every time they catch themselves talking to themselves, to pray instead.[11] This is what he believes Paul means in 1 Thessalonians 5:17 when he encourages the church to pray continually. The addicted minister has unsuccessfully handled life's issues by discussing them with self. This is especially true of Latino Pentecostal ministers, who can tend to be lone rangers and believe that their interpretation alone of what the Holy Spirit is doing and wants is sufficient to make wise decisions. Better results will come as the clergy in recovery now takes life issues to God in prayer, and by asking others for their help in prayer as well. Joseph Nowinski notes in his book *If You Work It, It Works* that there is a significant display of longer lengths of sobriety by those in the 12 Steps program that practice these spiritual disciplines such as prayer and meditation.[12]
>
> Step 11 discusses power. The Latino Pentecostal minister is a fighter. They preach about power. However, here the recovering clergy member learns the power of surrender. This surrender is to God's will. God honors humility. The minister draws near to God, and God draws near to the minister. There is a conscious contact taking place between God and the recovering addict. God is empowering the person in recovery to carry out His will.

---

[11] Davis, Martin M. *The Gospel and the 12 Steps: Following Jesus on the Path of Recovery*, (Martin M. David 2016), 142.

[12] Nowinski, Joseph, *If You Work it, It Works! The Science Behind 12 Step Recovery*, (Hazelden Publishing, Center City, MN, 2015), 141.

GOING DEEPER

RECOVERY QUESTIONS

1. Can you recall anytime that your life was heading in the wrong direction? If so, what brought you back? Describe this in detail.

2. How would you describe your beliefs about God and a Higher Power to a child?

3. What are your favorite sources of wisdom and knowledge about healthy values?

4. Has anything you ever read convinced you to change in some fundamental or deep way?

5. If you were stranded on a desert island with only one book, which book would you take? Why?

6. If you had only one week to live and unlimited resources, who would you gather around you and how would you pass the time?

7. Write out a complete form of what you would like your obituary to say.

8. What does the term God's will mean to you?

9. What are some ways you can assess whether or not you are carrying out God's will?

Now go over these answers with your sponsor or the person who is helping you.

CHAPTER 12 — PAY IT FORWARD

STEP 12 *Having had a spiritual awakening as the result of these Steps, I will carry this message to others battling pornography and lust, and practice these principles in all my endeavors.*

SCRIPTURES AND THOUGHTS

HEBREWS 4:12, *For the word of God is alive and active. Sharper than any double-edged sword, it penetrates even to dividing soul and spirit, joints and marrow; it judges the thoughts and attitudes of the heart.*

The recovering addict has had a spiritual experience because they have practiced godly biblical principles and God has honored this. Previously, the minister attempted to stop lusting and seeing pornography. However, it was superficial endeavors, not penetrating beyond thoughts and feelings. The person had not fully surrendered their will to God's will. This involved the person's soul, or flesh, thoughts-feelings-will, but it did not involve the person's spirit. However, after practicing these spiritual principles, the spirit was awakened and revived. Because they held onto these teachings, the truth set them free (John 8:32).

MATTHEW 28:19-20, *Therefore go and make disciples of all nations, baptizing them in the name of the Father and of the Son and of the Holy Spirit, and teaching them to obey everything I have commanded you. And surely I am with you always, to the very end of the age.*

As Jesus told His followers to go out and share the good news that they had heard and experienced, to disciple others and teach other people His commands and way of life, people in recovery are to do the same. This is the spirit of the program; carrying the message to others. This is done through discipline, mentoring, sponsoring and sharing our story with others.

GOING DEEPER

JESUS TELLS HIS FOLLOWERS TO go out and preach the good news. The recovering addict can share their story with others. However, given the nature of a recovery program for pornography addiction, the topic is sensitive. Anonymity and discretion must be practiced. Not everyone is receptive to speaking about sexual sin, especially sometimes in the Latino culture. Therefore, a good practice is what is found in the traditions of AA which is attraction rather than promotion.[13] Hopefully those that see a change in the recovering minister will be drawn.

A survey shows that more alcoholics were drawn to Alcoholics Anonymous through another active Alcoholics Anonymous participant (34%), as compared to a treatment facility, self-motivated, family, court order, a counselor, or a health professional.[14] As the recovering minister continues to practice these principles, God will use him or her to draw other people, especially ministers in need of recovery from sexual sin, lust and pornography addiction.

---

[13] *Alcoholics Anonymous Big Book,* 4th ed. (New York, NY: Alcoholics Anonymous World Services, 2002), 562.

[14] Nelson, James B., *Thirst: God and the Alcoholic Experience.* London: Westminster John Knox Press, 2004, 18.

GOING DEEPER

RECOVERY QUESTIONS

1. Have you been able to reach out to another recovering addict? If so, describe the situation and how it feels to you.

2. What kind of approach would you like to have had when you first started the program? How can you implement that type of approach in your life to others now?

3. What would you say if someone asked how the 12 Step program has worked for you?

4. How do you usually handle conflict? Do you know of any way to be more effective in conflict resolution? If so, how would you become more effective? What would be the steps?

5. How much time do you want to and are able to allow for working with others on their program? How will you go about setting that time aside?

6. Give some reasons why you are now ready to sponsor someone. Give some reasons why you think you might not be ready to sponsor someone. What will you do to overcome these challenges?

7. What outside resources can you call on when you need help as a sponsor?

8. How do you know if you are suited to helping another person work a 12 Step program?

Now go over these answers with your sponsor or the person who is helping you.

CONCLUSION

WHAT'S NEXT

SOBRIETY AND RECOVERY MUST BECOME a way of life for the recovering addict. The Latino minister has chosen a difficult profession. There is much pressure on his or her life. They must be deliberate about staying sober and living in recovery. As they teach others that Christianity must inundate every area of their lives, so the minister in recovery must apply the 12 Steps of recovery to every area of their lives. The Latino culture and Latino congregations can be a place for ministers to thrive, and it can be a place where addiction is empowered. The minister must be aware of their challenges and triggers and be proactive in maintaining a healthy ministry and a healthy way of life. Here are some tools to stay sober and live in recovery. They are as follows: attend meetings, work your steps, know your triggers, use your phone, be proactive, have a sponsor, be a sponsor, start a recovery ministry, share your story, seek counseling and refer others to counseling and a recovery ministry.

ATTEND MEETINGS

It is important for the person in recovery to attend 12 Steps meetings. Hopefully they can find a place where this workbook is being studied. There are other secular programs such as Sexaholics Anonymous. These can be found online, both in-person meetings and schedules for Zoom meetings. Many sponsors recommend that newcomers attend 30 meetings in 30 days to begin. This accustoms the newcomer to meetings and helps them through an arduous adjustment period.

WORK YOUR STEPS

In order for the person to experience true recovery, the Steps must be completed. Once completed, they must continue perpetually in the life of the minister and person in the recovery. James 1:22-25 tells us that a person must be a doer with what they have learned and not just a hearer, otherwise they are like someone who looks in a mirror, sees themselves, but when they walk away they forget what they have seen. So it is with the person in a recovery ministry. After they have worked the steps and completed the workbook, they must continue to

CONCLUSION

apply these principles in every area of life for the rest of their lives. Here are a few examples of how the minister can continue to live out the 12 Steps in ministry.

Step 1, I admit that I am powerless over ministry

Step 2, God can restore the ministry that He has given me to sanity

Step 3, I surrender all control of this ministry to God

Step 4, I examine my inventory in the good and bad of this ministry

Etc

These same steps can be applied to the minister's marriage, parenting, friendships, professional relationships, relationships with parishioners, and so on.

KNOW YOUR TRIGGERS

TRIGGERS are experiences that occur in the addict's daily life that detonate a negative emotional response. It can be a painful memory, a stressful experience, or resentment. It could be something from the past, present or future. The pornography addict experiences many visual triggers as well that arouse unhealthy sexual desires. All these begin the cycle of addiction and prompt the addict to act out. It is important for the minister in recovery to know his or her triggers.

A good thing to do is make a list of your triggers as you become aware of them. This way you know when you are being triggered and can understand that you are more susceptible to begin a cycle that will end in acting out. Share this list with your sponsor and other people in your program. Common to most 12 Steps programs, in Sexaholics Anonymous, one recovery tool is the acronym HALT. You need to be careful when you are *Hungry, Angry, Lonely*, and *Tired*.[15] As you continue to share your journey with other people in recovery, they might notice trigger patterns you have not picked up on. We all have blind spots. Your sponsor and recovery peers can help you see them.

---

15 *Sexaholics Anonymous,* (SA Literature 1989), 34.

CONCLUSION

PHONE CALLS

Some sponsors have those that they are sponsoring make 15 calls a day for the first 30 days. Calls are made to the sponsor and other people in recovery. Most meetings have a phone list. It is best to call people of the same gender. The calls need not be lengthy in time. A few minutes is sufficient. It is a time to check in and share where you are today.

It is highly recommended to call when you are being emotionally or sexually triggered. If you cannot speak on the phone because you are around others or you cannot use your phone during work hours, a text or email will suffice. A simple text stating *I surrender* will make a huge difference at that moment in the life of the person in recovery.

BE PROACTIVE

As time goes by, the recovering addict must become proactive. He or she has typically been reactive in addiction and most of the life. Now is the time to beat addiction to the punch. There is a saying in recovery; *Insanity is to do the same thing over and over again but expect different results.* Becoming proactive versus being reactive is a contrary action that will begin to change the destiny of the person in recovery. One example of this is on recovery phone calls. At first, people in recovery call their sponsor when they have failed or lost their sobriety. As time goes by, the addict will call their sponsor during the act, and then eventually call before beginning the cycle of acting out. The best way to stay sober is to identify triggering people and situations beforehand and call your sponsor before you are around that person or in that situation. You can surrender that person or situation in prayer with your sponsor, then check in again with your sponsor to see how the encounter went. *What did you learn? What will you do better or different next time?* Using the tools of recovery to be proactive can be applied to every area of life.

HAVE A SPONSOR

Having a sponsor is paramount to staying sober and recovering from any addiction. This is the person with whom you can share anything, ask for prayer, and with whom you can complete your 12 Steps work.

Many times, a person in recovery wants to dump everything on their spouse when they decide to sober up. Speaking with your spouse about pornography use, abuse or addiction is a delicate matter that if not handled properly can do much damage. Speak to your sponsor

CONCLUSION

before you speak to your spouse. Your spouse can screen what you should and should not share with your spouse.

Also, denominational leaders get involved in restoration processes for recovering ministers. Some ministers hide things from their denominational superiors for fear of losing their jobs and financial income. A sponsor can help screen these conversations as well. A minister should make their denominational leader aware of the situation. Hopefully these leaders will be graceful and wise. For the Latino minister that does not belong to a denomination, he or she needs a sponsor and peer recovery ministers to maintain accountability. A lack of accountability and isolation empower pornography addiction. For some Latino believers that came from the Catholic Church, direct access to God is novel and beautiful. However, a person needs other humans in their life to give an account, according to James 5:16. Confession is not a Catholic practice, it is a biblical practice. Make yourself accountable to another human being.

Many sponsors suggest finding a temporary sponsor. This person can preliminarily help you until you find a permanent sponsor. Some people in recovery go through a few sponsors until they find the right fit. The point is to have a sponsor. Unlike a pastor or parent that goes after the person in need, the person in recovery makes themselves accountable. They check in consistently with their sponsor, not waiting for the sponsor to check up on them. Nobody can want recovery for the person that needs it more than they do.

An example of this is what Pastor Rich Guerra teaches. In Luke 15 Jesus tells the story of the 3 lost: the lost sheep, coin and son. The sheep knew it was lost but did not know how to get back. Thus, the shepherd went after it. The coin did not know it was lost, nor did it know how to get back. Hence, the woman of the house went after it. The son however knew he was lost and knew how to return. Therefore, the father waited for the son's return. The father did not go looking for the son, but gladly received him when he came back. The minister addicted to pornography knows that they are lost and now through this workbook and other recovery tools knows how to return. The responsibility to recover is upon the addicted minister.

BE A SPONSOR

Being a sponsor is not difficult, and it will help keep you living in recovery. Dr. Jesse Miranda said that in ministry, everyone should have a Paul, a Barnabas and a Timothy in their life. You need a sponsor (Paul), you need a Barnabas or two (peers in recovery), and someone

CONCLUSION

to mentor in recovery (Timothy). As you are a better Jesus follower when you disciple a new convert, you are a better person of recovery when you sponsor someone. This person will keep you on your toes and your knees at the same time. They will motivate you to stay active in recovery, as you need to always be a few steps ahead of them.

A sponsor should have at least 30 days sober. A sponsor should have finished working their 12 Steps or be in the process of it. A sponsor should be ahead of the person being sponsored in time length of sobriety. A sponsor should sponsor people of the same gender. A sponsor should have their own sponsor. A sponsor should attend recovery meetings consistently. A sponsor should encourage the person they are sponsoring to form relationships with other people in recovery. A sponsor should maintain a sound relationship with safe and healthy boundaries with those that they sponsor.

At many recovery and 12 Steps meetings, the person in charge will ask those that are willing to temporarily sponsor someone to raise their hand. The newcomer has had a chance to hear the participation shares of different attendees. Hopefully the newcomer has connected or identified with one of the stories. If the person that shared their story raises their hand to temporarily sponsor someone, this is a good opportunity to ask that person to be their temporary sponsor, and possibly after a time their permanent sponsor. A person with experience can offer the newcomer their phone number, however it is best not to offer to be someone's sponsor. This is a humbling step that the newcomer should take themselves.

Rather than getting into the habit of offering advice to the person being sponsored, it is best to take a coach approach. Ask open-ended questions that begin with what, when, who, how, etc. The goal is for the person to recover from pornography, feel confident, and begin to sponsor others. Advice should be offered when the person asks their sponsor for it. A sponsor should make themselves available to help others, but sponsoring too many people at the same time can be overwhelming. Sponsoring a few people at a time is a prudent plan.

STARTING A RECOVERY MINISTRY IN YOUR MINISTERIAL CONTEXT

Pastors are encouraged to start a recovery ministry at their church. This can be for parishioners as well as members of the local community. This will be a great evangelistic opportunity as well as a fruitful avenue for connection with the local neighborhood. Missionaries can do the same in their local context wherever they minister. Although evangelists travel, they can introduce the concept of recovery ministry and make reference to this workbook

CONCLUSION

and other recovery ministries and principles in their presentation. Christian Counselors can recommend the workbook as well as facilitate gatherings where people can meet in a group setting to do the book work together. Hospital Chaplains can also open a recovery group for those that battle pornography addiction there at their facility.

SHARE YOUR STORY

As often as you can, share your story and journey of recovery with others. Because anything sexual can be a social taboo, discretion should be practiced. However, Psalm 107:2 says that those whom the Lord has redeemed should tell their story. Witness to others outside of church how God has freed you from pornography. Share with other ministers on how God has you on a recovery journey. Incorporate segments of your recovery story and the 12 Steps into your sermons and teachings. Be led by the Holy Spirit. As in John 3 Nicodemus came to Jesus at night in private, others will approach you privately. Be a safe person with whom they can identify. Share your recovery story.

COUNSELING

Counseling will help the recovering minister. Even though Latino ministers offer counseling for congregants, they do not always seek counseling for themselves, their marriages or families. Hispanic ministers need help just like anyone else, especially to fully recover from pornography use, abuse and addiction. Pornography use has been medicating pain and character flaws that need to be addressed. The counselor can offer a safe place not only for the minister but also for his or her family to say what possibly they have wanted to say to the minister in recovery but were afraid to say. Addiction is a family disease. Spouses and children of all ages can heal and relationships can be restored through counseling.

REFERRALS

It is important for all ministers to refer people in need to other resources and networks that can more effectively help them. Latino ministers have not always referred their congregants to other ministries or counselors. To go outside of the family or congregation for help can be a foreign concept to the Hispanic culture. However, it starts at the top. As the leader does, so will those that follow him or her. The spiritual leader that goes to counseling and or is part of a recovery ministry can break cultural taboos for those that follow them. Even mentioning something that they learned from counseling or sharing a recovery tool or concept in their sermon or teaching will open new doors to Latino congregants.

CONCLUSION

Para-church ministries, counseling centers and local churches should have a list of local help centers for different addictions and various types of trauma. It takes a village to help an addict in recovery and their family. Today, names, numbers and addresses are not needed like previously when making referrals. As a person goes on the internet, all they need is the name of the organization. Some of these are Celebrate Recovery, Overcomers Outreach, Alcoholics Anonymous, Narcotics Anonymous, Sexaholics Anonymous, and Breath of Life Foundation.

These tools work when you work them. There is power in Jesus' Name. He set me free, and He will do the same for you. Taken from AA, *A Vision for You*

> *Our book is meant to be suggestive only. We realize we know only a little. God will constantly disclose more to you and to us. Ask Him in your morning meditation what you can do each day for the man who is still sick. The answers will come, if your own house is in order. But obviously you cannot transmit something you haven't got. See to it that your relationship with Him is right, and great events will come to pass for you and countless others. This is the Great Fact for us. Abandon yourself to God as you understand God. Admit your faults to Him and to your fellows. Clear away the wreckage of your past. Give freely of what you find and join us. We shall be with you in the Fellowship of the Spirit, and you will surely meet some of us as you trudge the Road of Happy Destiny. May God bless you and keep you — until then.*[16]

---

16 *Alcoholics Anonymous Big Book,* 4th ed. (New York, NY: Alcoholics Anonymous World Services, 2002), 164.

www.ingramcontent.com/pod-product-compliance
Lightning Source LLC
Chambersburg PA
CBHW081211170426
43198CB00018B/2918